Everyday Problems

Everyday Problems
William Wegman

BRIGHTWATERS PRESS

ACKNOWLEDGMENTS:

Eve Darcy
Norman Fisher
Anita Grossman
Randy Johnsen
Archie Quarrier
Holly and Horace Solomon
Laurance Wieder

Design: Thomas Ridinger
Production: Red Ink

Printed in the United States of America

Library of Congress Catalog Card Number: 84-071459

ISBN 0-918305-04-7

BRIGHTWATERS PRESS
235 PARK AVENUE SOUTH
NEW YORK, NEW YORK 10003

FOR ELY AND GEORGE

Introduction

Sketches of ideas rather than renderings of things, William Wegman's drawings have a cartoon-like appearance that is finally misleading. Although a drawing like "The Odd Neighbor" objectifies a common defensive fantasy in a manner reminiscent of, say, William Steig's recent emblematic characters and some of Charles Addams' more spiteful studies, most of Wegman's drawings are noticeably lacking the escape hatch into popular superstition, or satirical disbelief, that makes the work of even good cartoonists pretty funny one day and ho-hum the next. Take the highway-exit motel whose signs promise HONOR, DIGNITY, and JUSTICE instead of cheap rates, free ice, and color TV: does the absence of traffic on the driveway to the office prove no one is interested, or have prospective clients been frightened away by a package deal they know they could never afford?

Wegman is one of the few artists in any medium who can keep a stylistic allusion light without trivializing either the original or his gloss, an ability due in part to his steadfast unwillingness to lock himself into a single drawing style. He recognizes "six or seven" basic styles of his own in the drawings, and the use of any one of them depends on such weighty considerations as which drawing instrument is closest to hand. When he appropriates another artist's style for a drawing or two, as in the drawing of "Two Philosophers" that lends a speculative twist to Matisse's sinuous line, he does so with the same non-committal and non-exploitative freedom with which he rummages around in his own repertory. The results are affectionate, graceful, and sharp—all the more so, perhaps, because he seems to have no aesthetic axes to grind.

Wegman stays fresh by thinking about his work as little as possible. A drawing may begin with an undertow of impulse that leads him to his work table or any other flat surface. A few lines or a splotch suggest an idea, then he associates freely until the drawing is finished—a matter of minutes, usually, but sometimes only seconds. For inspiration he occasionally skims through a few '50s-era grade-school textbooks and how-to manuals from the cartonfuls he salvaged from a Fourth Avenue dumpster one night shortly after moving to New York; more often, though, the ideas come right off the top of his head—from the heart, that is, of his concerns of the moment, to which history now and then

2 philosophers
worrying about everyday
problem.

supplies an unpredictable echo. "Toddler Holds Couple Hostage," for instance, is a 1978 flight of fancy that might have been canceled a year later, during the crisis in Teheran.

Wegman's lightness of touch is most readily apparent in drawings such as "Swing," "Flying Kite in Gymnasium," "Inhale/Exhale," and the haiku-like "No Ear is Perfectly Clean," inventions as bright and charming as soap bubbles blown into a summer sky. But this delicacy reveals an unexpected and perhaps more exhilarating strength when, instead of virtually supplying the subject, it is applied to material not often treated with such casual humor and elegance. Thus, in "Dancer Struck by Car," a leap of the imagination transforms an accident into a triumph of professional grace; and, in "Him & Her Sanitary Products," an impossibly flattened plane enables two profiles on an advertising sign to watch a man fall from a rooftop, and leads, like vertigo itself, into a fourth dimension where anything goes.

Or almost anything. Some matters of life and death are less mysterious and more malevolent than traffic accidents and crimes of passion because they involve too many contingencies for anyone to grasp, much less explain, and it is no coincidence that all of the overtly political drawings in this book are to be found in the last section. While some of the problems here are real because they could face anyone at any time, the political problems are real because they face everybody all the time, and their implications are so overwhelming that, in the drawings as in life, the healing parts usually played by wit, compassion, and sheer escape are left to irony.

Irony has limits, too, however, and one of them is reached in the drawing of a nuclear warhead about to hit a scene so desolated that it's easy to think, if only for the same mad millisecond it would take the payload to travel the last few feet, that the mess might just as well be wiped out. But who's kidding whom? Not William Wegman, in either case. He may be willing to entertain playful visions of venal cops and crooked politicians, of dangerous chemicals asway in suburban hammocks, and of trees decorated with "triangles of industrial waste," but he knows when to stop. That warhead has gone as far as art will take it. The rest is science fiction.

— Ron Horning

Little Problems

TRADING DOGS

NOT BAD

LOSE WEIGHT
by EATING less
through dieting

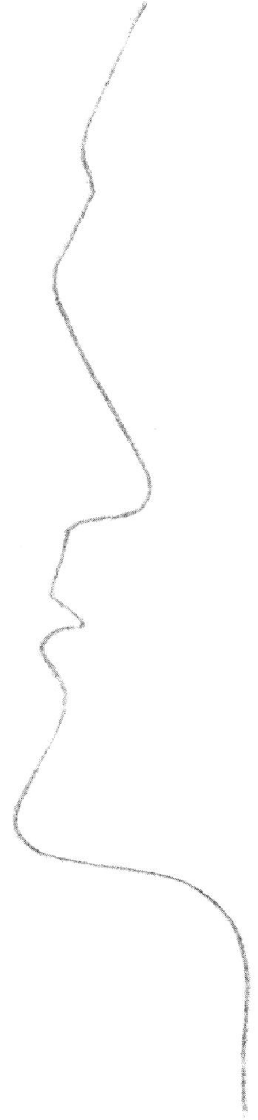

inhale

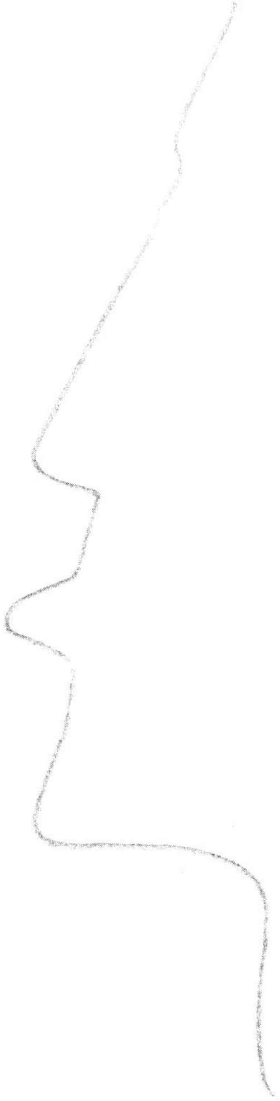

exhale

living in pick ups trucks

THE USUAL?
WHY NOT

flying kite in gymnasium

FITTING ROOM

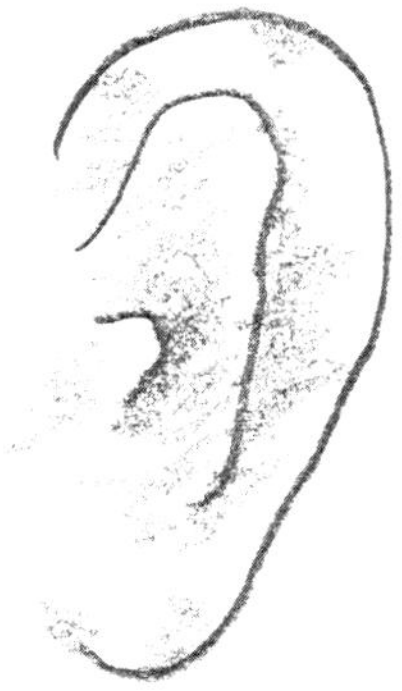

DIRTY EAR

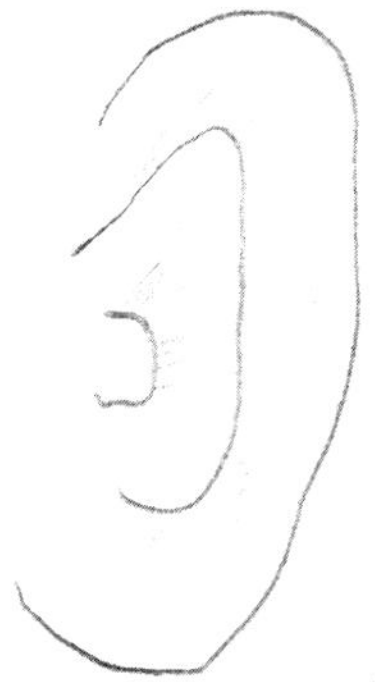

CLEANER EAR

NO EAR IS PERFECTLY CLEAN

LOCURA FURIOSA

Big Problems

BUG OFF LOU, HES NOT HURTING ME
GET YOUR ARM OFF MY SISTERS NECK

PARENTS SHOULD NOT
TRY TO FRIGHTEN
THEIR CHILD

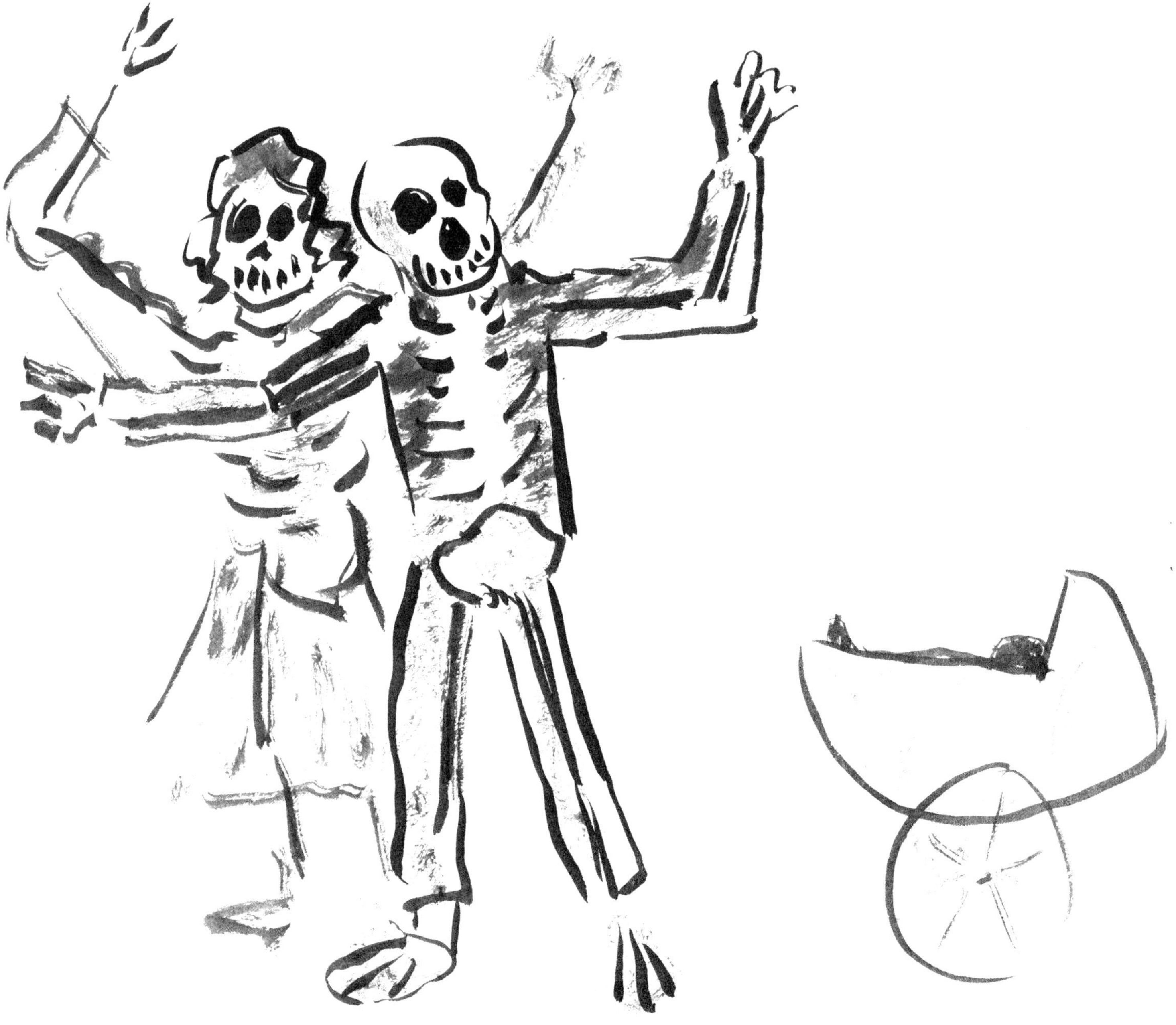

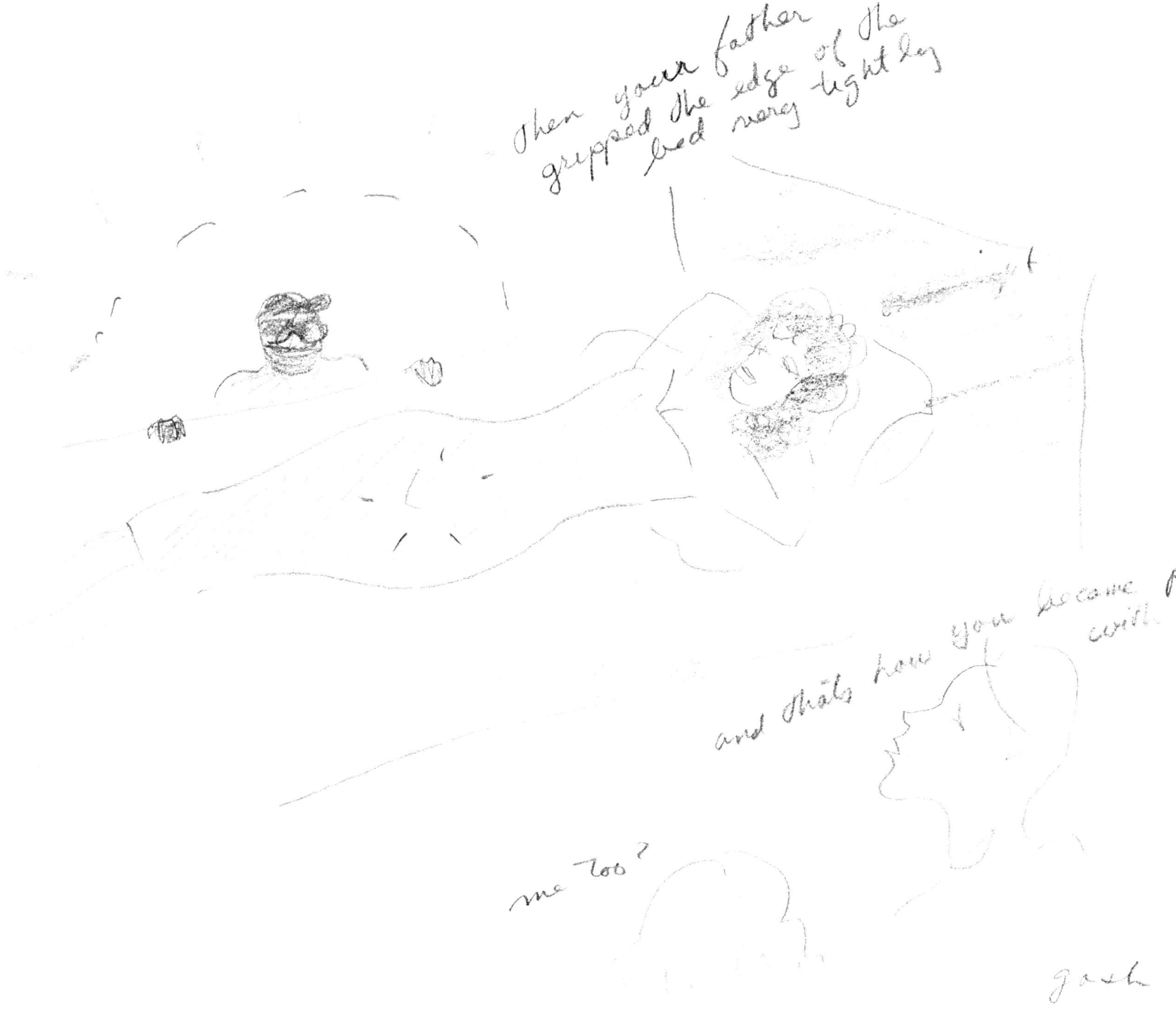
Then your father gripped the edge of the bed very tightly
and that's how you became pregnant with me?
me too?

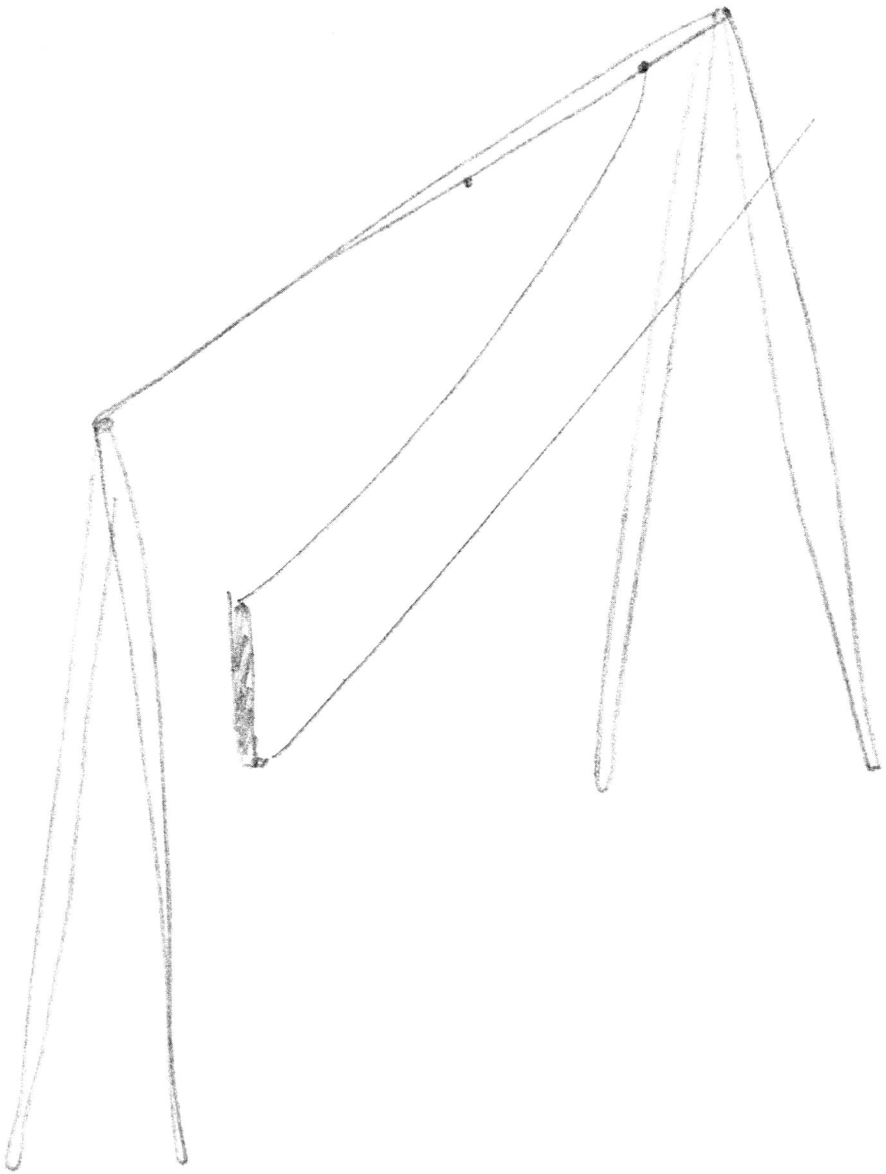

swing

CAN I HAVE THE CAR TONIGHT DAD?

GIRLS
MEN
DO THEY

how to pick up girls

I TOLD YOU NOT TO DO THAT
IT MAKES ME WANT TO DO IT MORE
GOD I LOVE IT WHEN SHE DOES IT

BE MY WIFE
ANYTHING

theres lead in
this ink
GET OUT
INK
INK

I trembled again today doctor

Dont worry

Real Problems

WELCOME TO MY HUMBLE ABODE

VETERANS
HOSPITAL

I'M NOT POSITIVE
BUT I THINK THIS IS
WHAT THEY WILL BE WEARING
IN THE NOT TOO DISTANT FUTURE.

dancer struck by car

Him Her
SANITARY PRODUCTS

State + local police working together

the odd neighbour

EAST AND WEST COOPERATING

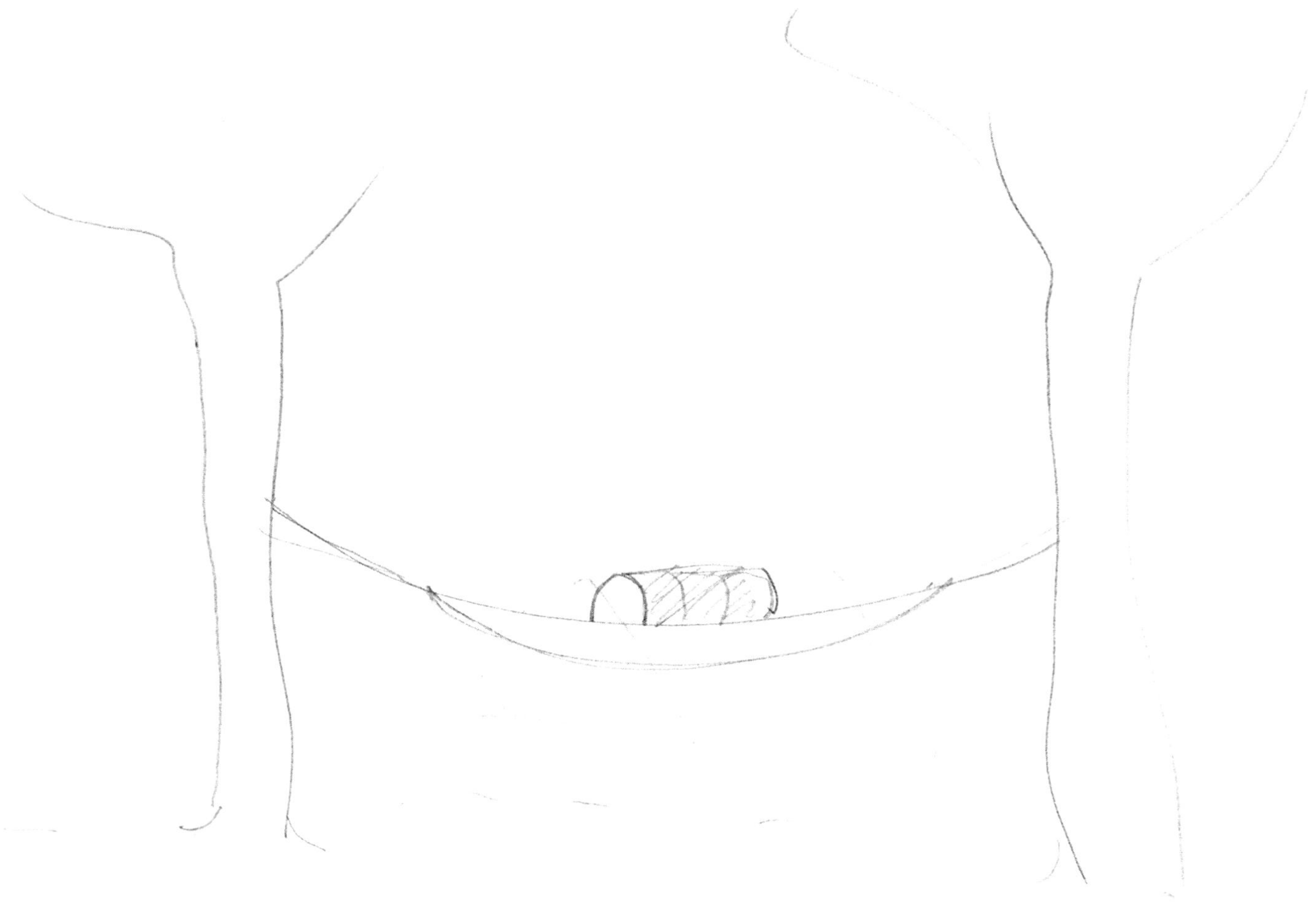

store dangerous chemicals
in hammock
cover with polyeth. tarp

American Horse Chestnut with Triangles of Industrial Waste

5$